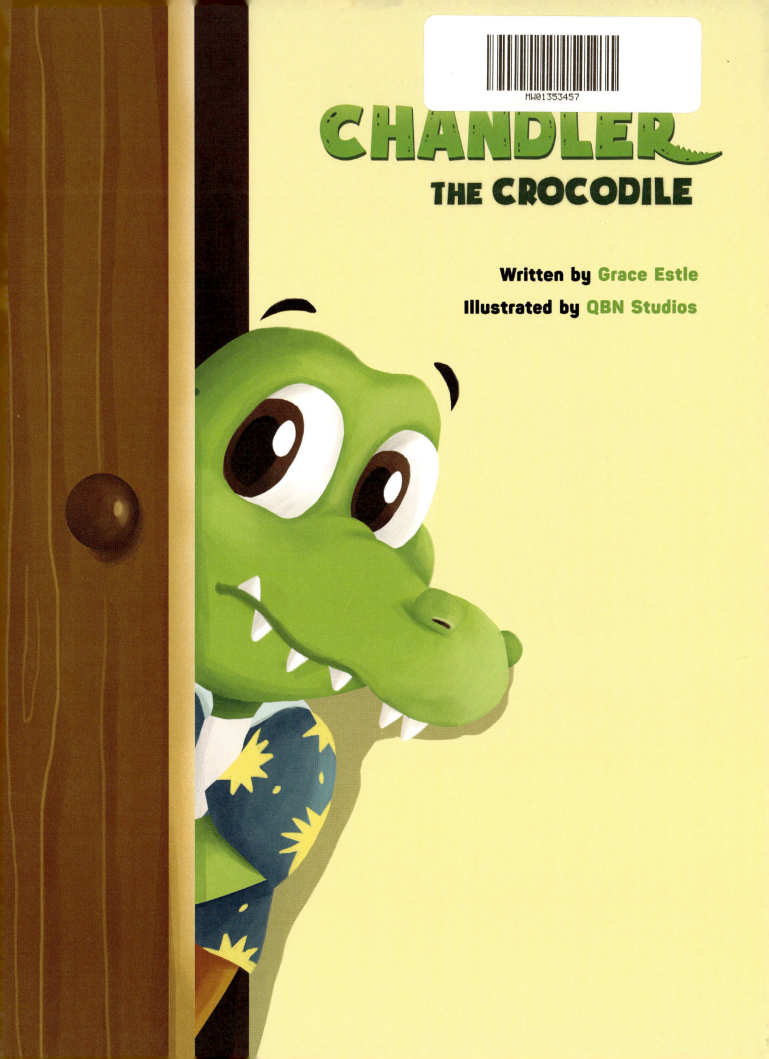
CHANDLER
THE CROCODILE

Written by **Grace Estle**
Illustrated by **QBN Studios**

graceestle.com
hello@graceestle.com

ISBN

978-1-7377084-0-7 - Print Hardcover
978-1-7377084-1-4 - Print Softcover
978-1-7377084-2-1 - eBook

Story © Grace Estle 2021

To Ma:

Thank you for showing me what true beauty is.

Chandler arrived at his new school. He looked at his classmates. They were fluffy bears with chocolate coats. Their eyes were as bright as blueberries. Their teeth were square and smooth.

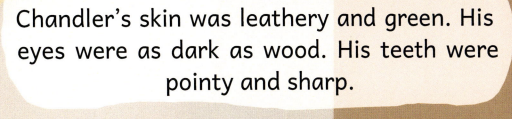

Chandler's skin was leathery and green. His eyes were as dark as wood. His teeth were pointy and sharp.

At lunch, no one ate with Chandler.

At recess, no one played with him.

At reading time, no one sat next to him.

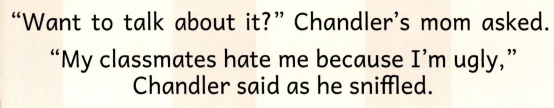

"Want to talk about it?" Chandler's mom asked.

"My classmates hate me because I'm ugly," Chandler said as he sniffled.

His mom stroked his head.
"You're the most handsome crocodile I know."

"I wish I had smaller teeth," Chandler said.

"Your teeth give you a beautiful smile."

Chandler's tears began to dry up. "But my eyes. They're too dark."

"You can spot a marble from a mile away."

"I wish I had a short tail like the bears, Mommy."

"Your tail makes you a powerful swimmer."

Chandler decided to use his gifts.

At lunch, he grinned at a boy.

Unfortunately, a tray of food got in his way.

At recess, Chandler spotted a butterfly. He tried to catch it for show and tell.

Unfortunately, a rock got in his way.

Chandler gave up. He threw a blanket over his mirror.

"How was your second day of school?" his mom asked.

"Horrible," Chandler cried. "You were wrong, Mommy. My gifts are useless. Everyone still hates me."

His mom hugged him. "Give it time, sweetheart. Why don't you show everyone your swimming talents at the back-to-school picnic?"

The picnic was on Saturday at the lake.
Chandler did a backflip off the diving board.

No one noticed.

Then Chandler noticed someone. The girl with the pink bow in her hair had swum out too far. Her arms flailed as she tried to stay afloat. No one could swim fast enough to save her.

Chandler dove to the lake's rocky bottom. He zipped so fast that he out swam the fish. Chandler caught the sinking girl on his back. Everyone clapped and cheered.

"Thank you, Chandler," the girl said.

Chandler beamed his pearly smile. The girl smiled too.

"My name is Maria. Would you like to build a sandcastle with me?"

The two headed over to a spot by the shore.
Chandler stared at his reflection.
He loved what stared back at him.

Grace Estle is from two worlds: the Philippines and the U.S. When she was four, her Filipina mom and American dad whisked her away from the Philippines to Ohio where she barely survived the arctic Midwest winters. Today, she thrives in the Florida heat and is dedicated to helping our youth celebrate the joy of uniqueness.

Catch up with Grace, and download story freebies now at graceestle.com.

QBN Studios is a small Illustration Studio located in Vernon Connecticut. Owners Quynh Nguyen and Christopher MacCoy are passionate about helping authors fulfill their dreams and bring their words to life. QBN Studio's goal is to create an immersive experience for their audiences to tumble headfirst into imaginary worlds.

Follow us on Instagram @qbnstudios for the latest updates on illustrations, books, and other projects.

Made in the USA
Middletown, DE
26 January 2022